puppy secrets

QEB

Camilla de la Bédoyère

Editor: Harriet Stone
Designer: Melissa Alaverdy

Copyright © QEB Publishing 2017

First published in the United States in 2017
by QEB Publishing
Part of The Quarto Group
6 Orchard, Lake Forest
CA 92630

A CIP record for this book is available from the Library of Congress.

ISBN: 978 1 68297 217 5

Printed in China

A PUPPY PROFILE on each breed contains information about **size**, **color**, and **energy level**.

PUPPY PROFILE

Medium

Usually black and white

*****

CONTENTS

AFGHAN HOUND

PUPPY PROFILE

Extra large

Any color

★★★★

An Afghan pup is small and cuddly, but as it grows it turns into a tall, elegant, and strong-minded dog. Afghans are fast runners and they can jump over fences, but this lovely pup won't go far!

SHHH, TOP SECRET!

When I'm older my hair will grow down to my toes!

 # BEAGLE

PUPPY PROFILE

 Medium

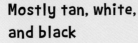 Mostly tan, white, and black

 ****

When a Beagle pup sniffs an interesting smell its ears prick up and it gets ready for action. Beagles have a great sense of smell and they often run around with their nose on the ground. They also like to bark and howl!

SHHH, TOP SECRET!

I love to steal your smelly socks, shoes, and slippers!

BICHON FRISE

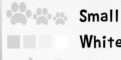

PUPPY PROFILE

Small

White

**

This little ball of white fluff wants to be everyone's best friend. He is full of character and energy. He is super smart, too! Bichons Frises have very thick fur, so they need to be brushed at least twice a week.

SHHH, TOP SECRET!

I like people to make a fuss over me, but don't spoil me or I'll be naughty!

BLOODHOUND

PUPPY PROFILE

Large

Black and tan or
liver and tan

★★★★

When a Bloodhound pup is born, it has just
a few wrinkles on its tiny face. Soon the
pup grows into a large dog and its wrinkles
grow too! Bloodhounds need plenty of space
and they love to follow interesting smells.

SHHH, TOP SECRET!

My secret is that I slobber
and drool...a lot!

BORDER COLLIE

PUPPY PROFILE

🐾🐾🐾 Medium

⬛⬛⬛⬜ Usually black and white

★★★★★

Border Collies are also called sheepdogs because they often live on farms. Collies love the outdoor life and they help farmers to move their sheep around. They are smart, easy to train, and very hardworking.

SHHH, TOP SECRET!

My favorite game is play-fighting with my brothers and sisters.

BOSTON TERRIER

PUPPY PROFILE

Medium

Brindle, black and white

***

This perfect playmate adores the indoor life and being with children. But when she's older she will enjoy a daily run outside. Boston Terriers are gentle dogs with a flat face, a short nose, and a big appetite!

SHHH, TOP SECRET!

My face needs washing every day, to keep me clean and healthy.

14

BRUSSELS GRIFFON

PUPPY PROFILE

 Small

Black and tan

 **

It's easy for a Brussels Griffon to fall in love with just one person. They become best friends forever and follow their "pet human" everywhere. But these dogs can also be stubborn when they want their own way.

SHHH, TOP SECRET!

My funny face sometimes makes me look grumpy, but I'm a happy pup!

CAVALIER KING CHARLES SPANIEL

PUPPY PROFILE

Small

Black and tan, black and white, ruby

**

When a spaniel is happy, it wags its tail. As this pup is always happy, his tail doesn't get much rest! Cavalier King Charles Spaniels like to chase and fetch, but most of all they like cuddles, kisses, and a warm lap.

SHHH, TOP SECRET!

I love to have my belly rubbed and my fur brushed!

CHIHUAHUA

PUPPY PROFILE

Small

Any color

**

Chihuahuas are the world's smallest dogs—most cats are bigger than them. This pup wears a warm coat when she goes outside and she may sulk if she gets wet. She likes to get her own way, always!

SHHH, TOP SECRET!

I am a big dog in a tiny dog's body! I can be protective and extremely entertaining!

COCKAPOO

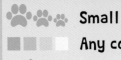

PUPPY PROFILE

 Small

Any color

★★★

This pup has one poodle parent and one Cocker Spaniel parent. That's why it's called a Cockapoo! It has all the energy and brains of a poodle, with the charm and cuteness of a spaniel.

SHHH, TOP SECRET!

I get sad when I'm on my own. I love people!

COCKER SPANIEL

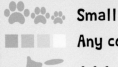

PUPPY PROFILE

Small

Any color

***

A Cocker Spaniel is the perfect pooch, with a lovely face, soft fur, and a happy nature. They are famous for being kind, gentle, and fun—and this young pup is already adorable in every way

SHHH, TOP SECRET!

My long ears get dirty, so someone has to clean them for me!

 # CORGI

PUPPY PROFILE

 Small

Red, sable, black, tan, often with white markings

***

Cute Corgis love everyone, and everyone loves them! They enjoy fun and games, and this pup will need lots of exercise when she's a little older. Corgis have short legs, a foxlike face, and they enjoy eating—sometimes a bit too much!

SHHH, TOP SECRET!

I can't run very fast, but that doesn't stop me from trying!

DALMATIAN

PUPPY PROFILE

Large

White with black or liver (dark brown) spots

*****

Dalmatians are the only dogs with spotted fur. They are full of energy, so they need plenty of space as well as good training. This puppy enjoys meeting other dogs and new people. He is friendly and smart.

SHHH, TOP SECRET!

I was pure white when I was born!

DOBERMANN

PUPPY PROFILE

Large

Usually black and tan or red

*****

A Dobermann is a bold, strong, and brave dog. It loves its family very much, but it's not so thrilled to meet strangers! This puppy enjoys some rough and tumble play, but he doesn't like the cold and he gets bored easily.

SHHH, TOP SECRET!

I may be big, but my feet are small and dainty.

ENGLISH BULLDOG

PUPPY PROFILE

Large

Usually a shade of brown, often with white markings

★★★

With big, wrinkled faces and short legs, these puppies are asking for love! Bulldogs are kind and gentle dogs that like to sleep and eat. They can get chubby if they don't go for a walk every day.

SHHH, TOP SECRET!

I don't like water and I can't swim.

FOX TERRIER

PUPPY PROFILE

 Medium

White, tan and black, or all white

★★★★

A Fox Terrier is a curious dog, always ready to explore and dig. These puppies are alert and friendly, and they enjoy being with children who are gentle with them. When it's older, this pup will adore lots of outdoor play.

SHHH, TOP SECRET!

I love to dig and get dirty!

FRENCH BULLDOG

PUPPY PROFILE

Small to medium

White, fawn, black, brindle

**

Most dogs love to swim, but French Bulldogs sink in water! They are very vocal dogs and they like to be with people all the time. These pups have such big eyes and ears that they are sometimes called "clown dogs".

SHHH, TOP SECRET!

Oops, I have a bit of trouble with gas! Can someone open a window please?

GERMAN SHEPHERD

PUPPY PROFILE

Large

Black and tan, all black, or all sable

*****

When a German Shepherd dog gets bored or lonely it starts to chew and bark. This puppy will work hard to please everyone. She is very smart and wants to be busy, helpful, and active much of the time.

SHHH, TOP SECRET!

I'm really good at fetching a Frisbee—it's my favorite toy!

GREAT DANE

PUPPY PROFILE

Extra large

Fawn, black, blue, or brindle

★★★★

This little cutie has three important jobs to do: eat, sleep, and grow! One day he will be enormous, with a giant-sized appetite to match. However big he gets, this Great Dane will always be sweet and gentle.

SHHH, TOP SECRET!

Soon I will be as big as you!

HUNGARIAN PULI

PUPPY PROFILE

 Medium

Black, white, gray, or fawn

★★★

It can take more than three years for a Puli pup's fur to reach its full length. When it's an adult dog, this pup will have long, thick strands of hair called cords. It's lucky this pup likes being groomed!

SHHH, TOP SECRET!

My hair makes me look much bigger than I really am.

42

 # HUSKY

PUPPY PROFILE

🐾🐾🐾 Medium

▪️▪️▪️▫️ Usually gray, blue, or black with white

★★★★★

Huskies come from the chilly north near the Arctic, so they like cold weather best. The cuddly pups look cute, but they can turn a room upside down when they are bored. Husky pups also like to dig holes!

SHHH, TOP SECRET!

You won't hear me bark much, but I love to howl!

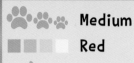 # IRISH SETTER

PUPPY PROFILE

 Medium

Red

★★★★★

This pretty pup will be young at heart for years to come. She loves to have fun and is always ready to spring into action when it's time for a little walk or game of fetch. Irish Setters are bold, loving, and beautiful.

SHHH, TOP SECRET!

I want to play all the time!

ITALIAN GREYHOUND

PUPPY PROFILE

Small

Almost any color

***

Bright-eyed and gorgeous, this pup is full of life and will be a loyal best friend. Italian Greyhounds are strong characters with graceful bodies. They adore running and chasing, but they love lying in the sunshine too.

SHHH, TOP SECRET!

I get cold in my short coat, so I like to snuggle up in warm places.

LABRADOODLE

PUPPY PROFILE

Medium

Any color

★★★★

Labradoodles are half Labrador Retriever and half poodle. This gorgeous pup will be easy to train and he will prove himself a loyal family member. He is full of energy though, so he'll expect playtime every day.

SHHH, TOP SECRET!

My curly hair can get into a terrible mess after I've been playing outside!

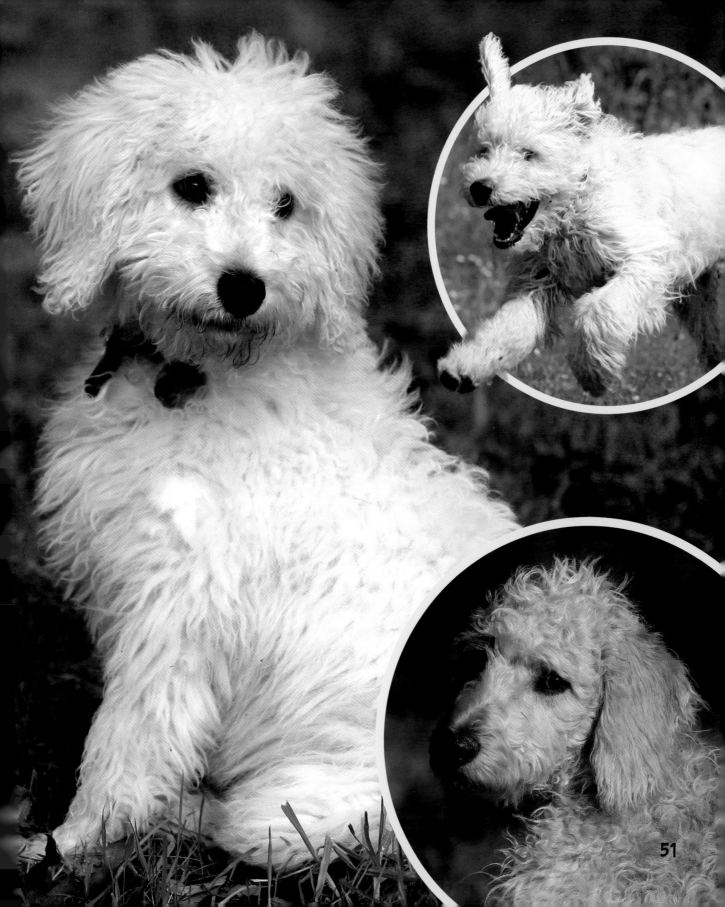

LABRADOR RETRIEVER

PUPPY PROFILE

 Medium

Golden, chocolate, or black

****

A Labrador has gentle eyes, a kind nature, and is a great fan of having fun! These pups have lots of energy, and even more love to give the people who look after them. Labrador pups need to chew, so this puppy needs lots of toys.

SHHH, TOP SECRET!

I know how to make everyone fall in love with me!

LHASA APSO

PUPPY PROFILE

🐾🐾🐾 Small

⬛⬛⬛⬜ Almost any color

🐾 **

A Lhasa Apso is very lively and acts like a puppy even when it grows up. This lovely pup needs careful training so she learns to be obedient, but she'll be gentle with children who are kind to her.

SHHH, TOP SECRET!

People call me stubborn, but I just like to do things my way!

 # MALTESE

PUPPY PROFILE

 Small

All white or white with black or lemon markings

**

Alert, smart, and friendly, this puffball of a pup needs lots of attention. Maltese dogs are devoted to their owners and, although they are small, tend to bark at strangers. These pups like short walks because they get tired quickly.

SHHH, TOP SECRET!

I don't like being called "cute". I'm simply brave and beautiful!

MASTIFF

PUPPY PROFILE

Extra large

Fawn, apricot, or black brindle

***

They may look glum, but these youngsters are cheerful pups with loads of energy. One day, they will be enormous—Mastiffs are some of the world's biggest dogs. They enjoy a cuddle, but watch out for the drool, the snoring, and the gas

SHHH, TOP SECRET!

I love my family, but I don't like strangers much.

OLD ENGLISH SHEEPDOG

PUPPY PROFILE

Large

Gray and white, blue and white, black and white

★★★★★

An Old English Sheepdog is the perfect dog for a family with lots of energy. These pets enjoy the outdoors where they bound through fields and woodlands. After a day out they need a bath and brush!

SHHH, TOP SECRET!

I love to splash in water and run through mud!

PAPILLON

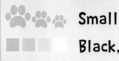

PUPPY PROFILE

 Small

Black, tan, sable, lemon, with white

*

Papillon pups aren't just gorgeous, they are als[o] smart and quick to learn tricks. They need lots [of] attention and they like being pampered. This p[up] enjoys playtime and running around in circles!

SHHH, TOP SECRET!

My name means "butterfly". I'm named after my cute ears!

PEKINGESE

PUPPY PROFILE

 Small

Almost any color

*

With big eyes and a little snub nose, this pup wins hearts everywhere he goes! He is brave and stubborn. He doesn't like being poked or having his hair or tail pulled. Pekes are small dogs with big personalities!

SHHH, TOP SECRET!

When I'm older my fur will grow long and silky.

POMERANIAN

PUPPY PROFILE

🐾🐾🐾 Small

▪▪▪▫ Any solid color

**

A Pomeranian pup is smart, playful, cute, and loving. She will stay that way all of her long life. This little dog loves its toys, and is always excited to be given a new one. She will need to be brushed at least twice a week.

SHHH, TOP SECRET!

My fluffy baby fur is super soft!

 # PUG

PUPPY PROFILE

🐾🐾 Small

Fawn, apricot, black, or silver

**

Pugs are snuggly, cuddly pups that love to be with people. They are eager to please, and this little puppy snorts and wheezes when it gets excited! Pugs like to be the center of attention.

SHHH, TOP SECRET!

Don't tell anyone, but I think cats are really cute!

ROTTWEILER

PUPPY PROFILE

Large

Black and tan

★★★★★

Rottweilers are very loyal dogs and these playful puppies will grow large and strong. Rottweilers need careful training so they learn how to behave around strangers and other animals. Their favorite game is fetch.

SHHH, TOP SECRET!

I'm a big, burly bundle of energy!

SAINT BERNARD

PUPPY PROFILE

 Extra large

White and tan
or brindle

***

A Saint Bernard is big, even when it's a pup! These dogs need more food than most dogs because of their great size. They come from cold places so they love to play in the snow and hate getting too hot.

SHHH, TOP SECRET!

I'm hungry, so hungry—
always hungry!

SAMOYED

PUPPY PROFILE

 Medium

■ ■ ■ □ White, cream, or biscuit

★★★

This adorable pup is called a Samoyed, or Sammy for short. He comes from cold places so his fur is long and warm and he needs lots of brushing. Samoyeds get bored quickly, so they need lots of playtime.

SHHH, TOP SECRET!

I have hairy toes! I grow thick hair on my feet so I can walk on snow.

SCHNAUZER

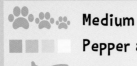

PUPPY PROFILE

Medium

Pepper and salt, black

***

This charming puppy is easygoing and loves being with children. He grows long fur around his muzzle, which quickly turns into a funny-looking mustache and beard! Schnauzers make perfect pets.

SHHH, TOP SECRET!

I'm a messy eater!

SCOTTISH TERRIER

PUPPY PROFILE

Small

Black or wheaten

**

Scottish Terriers love to play, but they don't like being teased. They are loyal, smart, and brave. These puppies are stubborn and like to get their own way, especially when they decide they want to dig!

SHHH, TOP SECRET!

I love walking and trotting, but I'm not a fast runner.

SHAR PEI

PUPPY PROFILE

Medium to large

Cream, fawn, sable, brown, black

***

Did you know that Shar Peis have blue-purple tongues? They have short fur that is easy to keep clean, and as the pups get bigger their skin grows into folds and wrinkles. This pup likes company, but bigger dogs scare him!

SHHH, TOP SECRET!

My wrinkles make me look sad, but I love life!

 # SHIH TZU

PUPPY PROFILE

 Small

Gold, gray, black often with white markings

**

Shih Tzu puppies have adorable faces with bright eyes—but you can't always see them behind their fluffy fur! Shih Tzus wheeze and snore, and they don't like the heat, but they are always friendly.

SHHH, TOP SECRET!

I'm also called a lion dog, but I can't roar no matter how hard I try.

STANDARD POODLE

PUPPY PROFILE

🐾🐾🐾 Medium

▪▪▪▫ Any solid color

★★★

There are three types of poodle: the Toy, the Miniature, and the Standard. The Standard Poodle is the biggest of the three, but this pup is still very cute! When she's older her fur might be clipped into shapes, called pom-poms.

SHHH, TOP SECRET!

I love swimming!

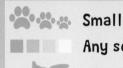 # TOY POODLE

PUPPY PROFILE

🐾🐾🐾 Small

⬛⬛⬛⬜⬜ Any solid color

🐕 **

A Toy Poodle pup is always busy learning about its owners and its home. Poodles are smart dogs that like being trained, and they have good memories. Even as puppies they need grooming to keep their fur clean and tidy.

SHHH, TOP SECRET!

My fur is so thick, curly, and fluffy that I'll need lots of haircuts!

WEIMARANER

PUPPY PROFILE

Large

Silver-gray

★★★★★

Weimaraners are called ghost dogs because they can move silently, slinking around their home and following their owners everywhere! This little pup will need to go to obedience classes or he might become quite a handful.

SHHH, TOP SECRET!

I'm so bouncy I often knock things over!

WEST HIGHLAND WHITE TERRIER

PUPPY PROFILE

Small

White

***

This Westie pup will melt the heart of everyone she meets! With a fun personality and a curious nature, Westies love to meet new people and visit new places. They are also happy relaxing at home.

SHHH, TOP SECRET!

I may be small, but I think I am the best dog in the world!

WHIPPET

PUPPY PROFILE

Medium

Any color

****

A Whippet is everyone's friend, but these sprightly dogs don't always get along with cats! This pup will need lots of exercise when he's older. A lonely Whippet can quickly become sad, so he needs lots of hugs.

SHHH, TOP SECRET!

I always smell sweet, even when my fur gets wet!

YORKSHIRE TERRIER

PUPPY PROFILE

 Small

Steel-blue body with pale face and legs

 *

This teeny-tiny pup is called a Yorkie for short. Although it's a bundle of fun, a Yorkie pup is so small and delicate that it needs to be handled very gently. When it's older, this pup will adore having its long hair brushed.

SHHH, TOP SECRET!

I'm a very vocal pup and make all sorts of funny noises when I'm excited!

Picture Credits

fc= front cover, bc=back cover, bg=background, t=top, b=bottom, l=left, r=right, c=center

All images are courtesy of © 2016 Bob & Pam Langrish KA9 Photo, with the exception of the following.

Alamy: 16c GROSSEMY VANESSA, 84c Tierfotoagentur

Dreamstime: 35r © Robert Malota, 35bl © Cynoclub, 43tc © Csaba Vanyi, 43bl © Lunja87, 85t © Deborah Calnan

Getty: fc Joelle Sedlmeyer

iStock Photo: 74c elenaleonova

Shutterstock: bc Grigorita Ko, 2-3bg Grigorita Ko, 4c otsphoto, 5l otsphoto, 5tr otsphoto, 5br Peter Lang, 15tr April Turner, 15c Siva Nattharom, 21tr tsik, 21br gillmar, 26c Grigorita Ko, 29br otsphoto, 32c otsphoto, 33tr WilleeCole Photography, 33c Grigorita Ko, 33bl Grigorita Ko, 34c Olga Kurguzova, 35t Maksym Gorpenyuk, 38c Grigorita Ko, 39tr Lenkadan, 39c Waldemar Dabrowski, 39br Grigorita Ko, 40c Rey Kamensky, 41tr Ricantimages, 41c Guy J. Sagi, 41br Eric Isselee, 42c BORINA OLGA, 43br BORINA OLGA, 44c ANURAK PONGPATIMET, 45tr SashaS Skvortcova, 45l Sbolotova, 45br dezi, 46c anetapics, 48c Akbudak Rimma, 49tr Linn Currie, 49l Omelianenko Anna, 50c Marie Dolphin, 52c Okeanas, 53tr DTeibe Photography, 53c Mila Atkovska, 56c NEO80, 57c Eric Isselee, 58c rokopix, 59c rokopix, 59br Robynrg, 60c Grigorita Ko, 61tr Serge Vero, 61br Kate Grishakova, 62c Zuzule, 63c Liliya Kulianionak, 64c Happy monkey, 65tr Sarut Chaprasert, 65c Jagodka, 66c YamabikaY, 67tr YamabikaY, 67c Natalia Fadosova, 72c Grigorita Ko, 73c MirasWonderland, 73tr Grigorita Ko, 75tr Abramova Kseniya, 75c Dora Zett, 75br Dora Zett, 78c Ninelle, 79t Stephen Dukelow, 79c Anna Tkach, 79br eAlisa, 80c Liliya Kulianionak, 81t jacotakepics, 81br Angel Sallade, 81bl Zuzule, 83t Eric Isselee, 83bl ninii, 83br Nagel Photography, 85bl JLSnader, 85br Andreas Gradin, 86c Jne Valokuvaus, 87tr KellyNelson, 87c JStaley401, 88c DragoNika, 89tl Zuzule, 89cl Csanad Kiss, 89r DragoNika, 92c Laila Kazakevica, 93tr cynoclub, 93c Liliya Kulianionak, 94c tsik, 95tr tsik, 95c Labrador Photo Video, 96c Grigorita Ko